STORY:
KERRI O'HERN AND GINI HOLLAND

ILLUSTRATIONS:
D. MCHARGUE

WORLD ALMANAC® LIBRARY

FREE MANDELA!

NELSON MANDELA SPENT 27 YEARS IN PRISON BECAUSE HE BELIEVED IN FREEDOM FOR ALL! DURING HIS YEARS IN PRISON, HE BECAME A SYMBOL OF THE STRUGGLE AGAINST THE WHITE GOVERNMENT IN SOUTH AFRICA. WHEN HE WAS FINALLY RELEASED, THOUSANDS OF SUPPORTERS WERE THERE TO GREET HIM. PEOPLE AROUND THE WORLD CELEBRATED THE END OF THIS HORRIBLE PERIOD IN SOUTH AFRICA'S HISTORY. THE END OF HIS YEARS IN JAIL MEANT THE BEGINNING OF FREEDOM FOR ALL BLACK SOUTH AFRICANS!

IT ALL BEGAN 400 HUNDRED YEARS AGO . . .

DURING THE 1600S, WHITE EUROPEANS BEGAN TO SETTLE IN SOUTH AFRICA. THEY CAME BECAUSE SOUTH AFRICA HAD RICH LAND, GOLD, AND DIAMONDS. THE WHITE SETTLERS FORCED THE NATIVE AFRICANS FROM THEIR LANDS. SOON THE WHITES HAD CONTROL OVER MOST OF THE LAND. THEY CALLED THE AREA THE "CAPE COLONY."

CHILDREN OF THE DUTCH, GERMAN, AND FRENCH SETTLERS WERE CALLED AFRIKANERS. THEY CREATED A LANGUAGE CALLED AFRIKAANS.

WITHOUT THEIR LANDS TO RAISE FOOD AND ANIMALS ON, THE AFRICANS COULD NOT SUPPORT THEMSELVES. THE WHITES FORCED THE AFRICANS TO WORK IN THE GOLD AND DIAMOND MINES.

IN 1890 CECIL RHODES, FOUNDER OF KIMBERLY DIAMOND MINES, BECAME PRIME MINISTER OF CAPE COLONY. HE ANNOUNCED THAT VOTERS HAD TO READ.

KIMBERLY DIAMOND MINES

MOST BLACK AFRICANS COULD NOT READ, SO THEY COULD NOT VOTE.

BALLOT
VOTE

VOTE HERE!
6AM to 7PM

WITHOUT A VOTE, THEY COULD NOT PARTICIPATE IN POLITICS. THIS MEANT THAT THE OPINIONS OF BLACKS AND OTHER PEOPLE OF COLOR, OR NONWHITES, DID NOT MATTER IN SOUTH AFRICA.

WHILE THE WHITES GAINED WEALTH, THE ORIGINAL AFRICANS GREW POORER AND POORER.

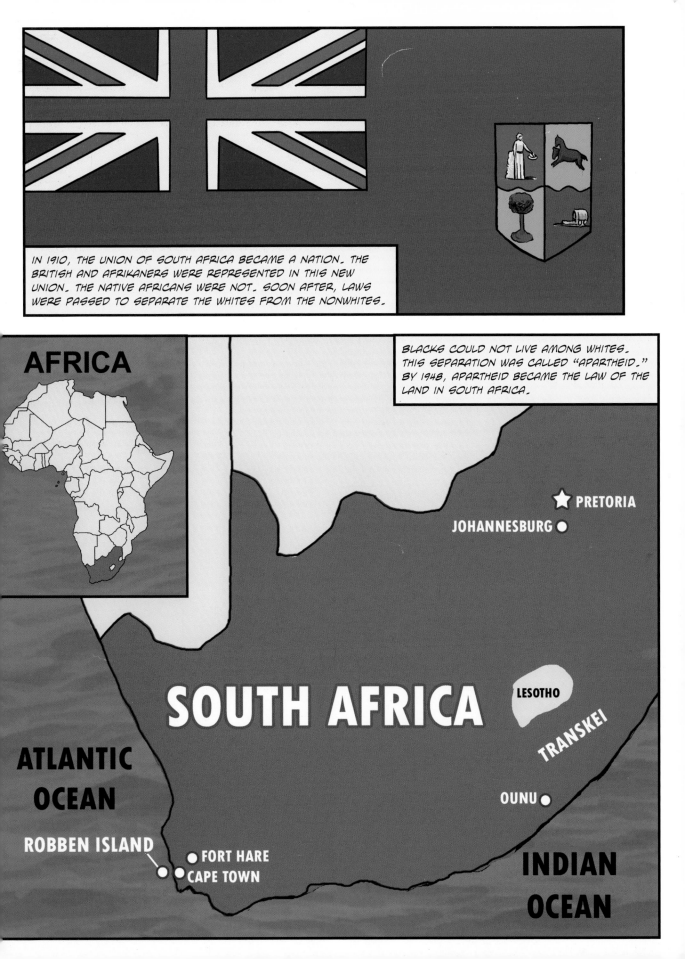

IN 1910, THE UNION OF SOUTH AFRICA BECAME A NATION. THE BRITISH AND AFRIKANERS WERE REPRESENTED IN THIS NEW UNION. THE NATIVE AFRICANS WERE NOT. SOON AFTER, LAWS WERE PASSED TO SEPARATE THE WHITES FROM THE NONWHITES.

BLACKS COULD NOT LIVE AMONG WHITES. THIS SEPARATION WAS CALLED "APARTHEID." BY 1948, APARTHEID BECAME THE LAW OF THE LAND IN SOUTH AFRICA.

AFRICA

★ PRETORIA
JOHANNESBURG ●

SOUTH AFRICA

LESOTHO

TRANSKEI

ATLANTIC OCEAN

OUNU ●

INDIAN OCEAN

ROBBEN ISLAND

● FORT HARE
● CAPE TOWN

NOTICE
THIS PUBLIC BEACH IS CLOSED TO ALL NON-WHITES

THERE WERE MANY MORE NONWHITES IN SOUTH AFRICA THAN WHITES. YET THE WHITE POPULATION WAS ABLE TO CONTROL THE NATION. HOW WAS THIS POSSIBLE? . . .

NOTICE
THIS PUBLIC BEACH IS CLOSED TO ALL NON-WHITES

. . . THROUGH TAKING THE AFRICANS' LAND AND ITS RESOURCES, THROUGH NOT ALLOWING THEM TO VOTE, AND KEEPING THEM OUT OF POLITICS.

UNDER APARTHEID, WHITES HAD MORE POWER AND MONEY THAN NONWHITES. ALL WHITES COULD VOTE. ALL WHITES COULD OWN PROPERTY. ALL WHITES COULD TRAVEL FREELY WITHIN SOUTH AFRICA.

UNDER APARTHEID, NONWHITES HAD TO LEAVE MOST CITIES BY SUNSET OR BE ARRESTED. THEY HAD TO HURRY OUT OF THE CITY AFTER WORK. UNDER APARTHEID, NONWHITES COULD NOT RECEIVE A GOOD EDUCATION.

THE MAN WHO EVENTUALLY ENDED APARTHEID WAS BORN IN 1918. NELSON MANDELA GREW UP IN MVEZO, A SMALL THEMBU VILLAGE IN SOUTH AFRICA. MANDELA'S FATHER WAS A TRIBAL CHIEF. THE THEMBU KINGDOM IS ONE OF MANY TRIBAL GROUPS IN SOUTH AFRICA. AS A CHILD, NELSON WAS TAUGHT HOW TO BE A TRIBAL LEADER.

ROLIHLAHLA, THE NAME GIVEN TO MANDELA AT BIRTH, MEANS "TROUBLE MAKER." AS A CHILD, MANDELA WAS TAUGHT AFRICAN CULTURE AND TO BE A LEADER OF HIS TRIBE.

MANDELA ALSO ATTENDED A WHITE-RUN SCHOOL. THERE, HE LEARNED ABOUT EUROPEAN CULTURE.

HIS FIRST TEACHER AT THIS SCHOOL GAVE HIM A NEW NAME—NELSON.

WHEN MANDELA GOT OLDER, HE DECIDED TO MOVE TO JOHANNESBURG. HE HAD TO BREAK "APARTHEID LAWS" TO GET THERE. NONWHITES WERE NOT ALLOWED TO TRAVEL FROM TOWN TO TOWN.

MANDELA WORKED IN THE MINES WHEN HE GOT TO JOHANNESBURG.

MINE SHAFT 67-B

HE THOUGHT THE CITY WOULD BE FULL OF MONEY AND BRIGHT LIGHTS. INSTEAD, ALL HE SAW WAS HOW HORRIBLY BLACK PEOPLE WERE TREATED.

A GOLD MINE RESEMBLES A WAR TORN BATTLEFIELD.

MANDELA DECIDED TO FIGHT AGAINST THE RACISM IN HIS COUNTRY. HE STUDIED LAW AND GOT A JOB WITH A LAW FIRM. THIS FIRM DID NOT AGREE WITH "APARTHEID LAWS." THEY WERE WILLING TO HIRE A BLACK LAWYER.

SOON, MANDELA JOINED THE AFRICAN NATIONAL CONGRESS (ANC). THIS GROUP FOUGHT TO END APARTHEID.

HE ALSO HELPED FORM A NEW DIVISION OF THE ANC FOR YOUNGER VOLUNTEERS. THIS BOLDER GROUP WAS CALLED THE YOUTH LEAGUE.

IN 1952, NELSON MANDELA AND OLIVER TAMBO OPENED THE COUNTRY'S FIRST BLACK LAW FIRM. UNDER APARTHEID, THEY DID NOT HAVE PERMISSION TO PRACTICE LAW. BY BEING BLACK AND PRACTICING LAW, THEY WERE ACTUALLY BREAKING THE LAW.

MANDELA AND MEMBERS OF THE ANC WARNED THE WHITE GOVERNMENT THAT IT MUST END ALL APARTHEID LAWS. THE WHITE GOVERNMENT ANSWERED WITH EVEN HARSHER LAWS.

THEY BANNED BLACK NEWSPAPERS AND ARRESTED OVER 8,500 PEOPLE. ONE OF THEM WAS MANDELA. HE WAS RELEASED, BECAUSE HE WAS NONVIOLENT.

NOTICE

THIS BUSINESS CLOSED UNTIL FURTHER NOTICE

BY ORDER OF POLICE ORDINANCE 345-KER

IN 1960, A PEACEFUL GROUP WAS PROTESTING SOME OF THE APARTHEID LAWS. SOUTH AFRICAN POLICE STARTED SHOOTING THE PROTESTORS. MOST WERE SHOT IN THE BACK. CLEARLY, THESE PROTESTERS HAD BEEN TRYING TO ESCAPE THE POLICE, NOT ATTACK THEM.

MANDELA REALIZED THAT PEACEFUL PROTESTS DID NOT WORK. UPSET, HE HELPED FORM A NEW GROUP. THIS NEW GROUP PLANNED TO BOMB EMPTY GOVERNMENT BUILDINGS. THEY HOPED TO DEMOSTRATE THEIR UNHAPPINESS WITH APARTHEID LAWS.

NELSON MANDELA WAS ARRESTED IN 1962 FOR HIS ACTIONS PROTESTING APARTHEID. HE WAS SENTENCED TO FIVE YEARS OF HARD LABOR IN PRETORIA PRISON.

GUILTY!

I HAVE CHERISHED THE IDEAL OF A DEMOCRATIC AND FREE SOCIETY IN WHICH ALL PERSONS LIVE TOGETHER IN HARMONY AND WITH EQUAL OPPORTUNITIES. . . . IT IS AN IDEAL WHICH I HOPE TO ACHIEVE. BUT IF NEEDS BE, IT IS AN IDEAL FOR WHICH I AM PREPARED TO DIE.

WHILE SERVING THESE FIVE YEARS, MANDELA WAS ACCUSED OF ANOTHER ACT AGAINST THE GOVERNMENT. DURING HIS TRIAL, MANDELA DEFENDED THE GOALS OF THE ANC.

HE DID NOT WIN THE TRIAL. HE WAS SENTENCED TO LIFE IN PRISON. NELSON MANDELA SPENT MANY DAYS BREAKING LIMESTONE ROCK IN THE HOT SUN.

IN 1964, MANDELA WAS MOVED TO A PRISON ON ROBBEN ISLAND. HE WORKED ALL DAY, AND HIS MUSCLES HURT ALL THE TIME. BUT HE DID NOT GIVE UP HIS ANTI-APARTHEID FIGHT.

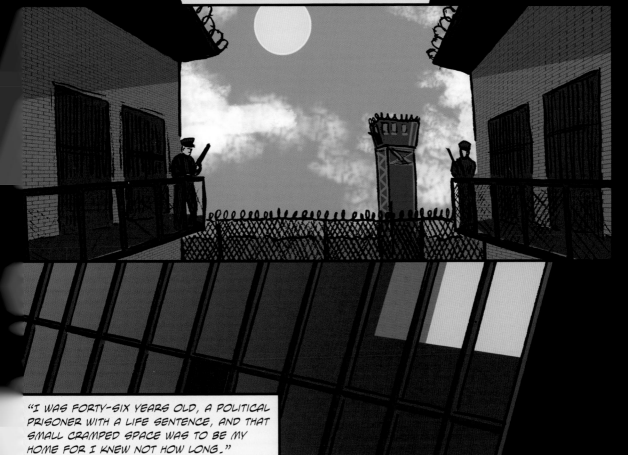

"I WAS FORTY-SIX YEARS OLD, A POLITICAL PRISONER WITH A LIFE SENTENCE, AND THAT SMALL CRAMPED SPACE WAS TO BE MY HOME FOR I KNEW NOT HOW LONG."

—NELSON MANDELA

MY DEAREST HUSBAND...

PRISON LIFE MEANT NO VISITORS AND CENSORED MAIL! MANDELA COULD NOT EVEN SEE HIS WIFE OR CHILDREN FOR SEVERAL YEARS! HIS WIFE WOULD WRITE, BUT THE GUARDS CUT OUT MANY OF HER WORDS.

ARGH! THAT WAS A LETTER FROM MY WIFE WINNIE.

MANDELA'S LAW PARTNER, OLIVER TAMBO, TRAVELED TO MANY COUNTRIES. OLIVER GATHERED SUPPORT TO END APARTHEID. HE SPOKE TO THE UNITED NATIONS (UN), A GROUP OF SEVERAL NATIONS THAT DISCUSSES WORLD PROBLEMS.

IN 1973, THE UN CALLED APARTHEID A CRIME. THIS GROUP'S OPINION WAS IMPORTANT TO THE WORLD. THE WORLD FOUND OUT HOW HORRIBLE SOUTH AFRICA'S GOVERNMENT WAS.

IN 1976, A REBELLION BEGAN IN SOWETO. THIS WAS A POOR, CROWDED AREA. MOST OF THE NONWHITES WHO WORKED IN NEARBY JOHANNESBURG HAD TO LIVE THERE. THIS REBELLION STARTED PEACEFULLY. A GROUP OF STUDENTS WANTED MANDELA SET FREE.

THE STUDENT PROTESTORS ALSO WANTED A BETTER EDUCATION. SOUTH AFRICAN LAW STATED THAT SCHOOL BE TAUGHT IN AFRIKAANS. BUT MOST BLACK AFRICANS DID NOT SPEAK AFRIKAANS WELL SO THEY HAD TROUBLE UNDERSTANDING THEIR LESSONS. WITHOUT A GOOD EDUCATION, THEY HAD NO HOPE OF LIVING A BETTER LIFE.

THE POLICE STARTED FIRING GUNS AT THE STUDENTS. THE STUDENTS RAN! THEY FOUGHT BULLETS WITH STONES AND BOOK BAGS. THE STUDENTS' PARENTS JOINED THE FIGHT TOO.

THREE DAYS LATER, OVER 1,000 PROTESTORS HAD BEEN SHOT! YET THE GOVERNMENT BLAMED THE VIOLENCE ON THE STUDENTS.

FREE MANDELA

RIOTS SPREAD TO EIGHT OTHER TOWNS. NONWHITES WANTED A BETTER LIFE IN SOUTH AFRICA. EACH YEAR, THESE PROTESTS GOT WORSE. MANDELA WROTE TO THE GOVERNMENT ASKING THEM TO WORK WITH THE ANC. THE GOVERNMENT IGNORED HIS LETTERS.

YOU MUST HELP US!

FINALLY, THE SOUTH AFRICAN GOVERNMENT REALIZED THAT IT NEEDED MANDELA'S HELP.

THE REST OF THE WORLD KNEW APARTHEID CONTINUED IN SOUTH AFRICA. IN PROTEST, MANY COUNTRIES STOPPED BUYING GOODS FROM SOUTH AFRICA. THE U.S. GOVERNMENT BANNED SOUTH AFRICAN AIRLINES FROM LANDING ITS PLANES IN THE UNITED STATES.

MEANWHILE, PEOPLE AROUND THE WORLD CELEBRATED MANDELA'S SEVENTIETH BIRTHDAY. A ROCK CONCERT RAISED MONEY FOR THE ANTI-APARTHEID MOVEMENT.

IN OCTOBER OF 1989, SOUTH AFRICA ELECTED F. W. DE KLERK AS PRESIDENT. HE PROMISED TO LOOK FOR WAYS TO END THE VIOLENCE.

HE MET WITH MANDELA IN DECEMBER 1989. A FEW MONTHS LATER, HE CHANGED SOME OF THE APARTHEID LAWS. ALL RACES WOULD NOW BE ABLE TO VOTE. THEN, HE ANNOUNCED THAT MANDELA WOULD BE SET FREE!

ON FEBRUARY 11, 1990, NELSON MANDELA WAS FREED FROM PRISON! HE WAS HAPPY TO SEE HIS WIFE AGAIN. NOW HE WANTED TO HEAL HIS COUNTRY.

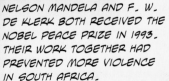

NELSON MANDELA AND F. W. DE KLERK BOTH RECEIVED THE NOBEL PEACE PRIZE IN 1993. THEIR WORK TOGETHER HAD PREVENTED MORE VIOLENCE IN SOUTH AFRICA.

MANDELA RAN FOR PRESIDENT. THIS WAS THE FIRST NATIONAL ELECTION ALLOWING BLACK AFRICANS TO VOTE.

HE BECAME PRESIDENT OF SOUTH AFRICA IN 1994. MANDELA CHOSE TO SERVE ONLY TWO TERMS.

FOR YEARS, FEW ROADS AND TELEPHONES LINKED BLACK AFRICANS TO EACH OTHER. NOW, THE COUNTRY NEEDED TO BUILD A SYSTEM OF ROADS, RAILROADS, AND TELEPHONE LINES. BETTER EDUCATION FOR EVERY CITIZEN WAS NEEDED FOR THIS NATION TO GROW. MANDELA STARTED SOUTH AFRICA ON THE PATH TO THESE GOALS.

WE SHALL BUILD THE
SOCIETY IN WHICH ALL SOUTH
AFRICANS, BOTH BLACK AND WHITE, WILL
BE ABLE TO WALK TALL, WITHOUT ANY FEAR
IN THEIR HEARTS . . . A RAINBOW
NATION AT PEACE WITH ITSELF
AND THE WORLD.

ALTHOUGH NELSON MANDELA'S PRESIDENTIAL
YEARS ARE OVER, HE REMAINS A SYMBOL OF
FREEDOM. HIS VISION AND SELF-SACRIFICE
CONTINUE TO INSPIRE PEOPLE THROUGHOUT
THE WORLD.

MORE BOOKS TO READ

Modern African Political Leaders. R. Kent Rasmussen (Facts on File)

Apartheid in South Africa. David Downing (Heinemann Library)

Nelson Mandela. Reggie Finlayson (Lerner Publications)

Nelson Mandela. Rookie Biographies (series). Karmina Grant (Scholastic Library)

Nelson Mandela. Trailblazers of the Modern World (series). Gini Holland
   (World Almanac Library)

WEB SITES

Freedom Heroes
myhero.com/myhero/hero.asp?hero=nelsonMandela

Go Places: South Africa
www.timeforkids.com/TFK/specials/goplaces/0,12405,384364,00.html

Leaders & Revolutionaries
www.time.com/time/time100/leaders/profile/mandela.html

The Long Walk of Nelson Mandela
www.pbs.org/wgbh/pages/frontline/shows/mandela

World Almanac for Kids
www.worldalmanacforkids.com/explore/nations/southafrica.html

Please visit our web site at: www.worldalmanaclibrary.com
For a free color catalog describing World Almanac® Library's
list of high-quality books and multimedia programs,
call 1-800-848-2928 (USA) or 1-800-387-3178 (Canada).
World Almanac® Library's fax: (414) 332-3567.

Library of Congress Cataloging-in-Publication Data

O'Hern, Kerri.
    Nelson Mandela / Kerri O'Hern and Gini Holland.
        p. cm. — (Graphic biographies)
    Includes bibliographical references.
    ISBN 0-8368-6197-3 (library binding)
    ISBN 0-8368-6249-X (softcover)
    1. Mandela, Nelson, 1918—Juvenile literature. 2. Presidents—
South Africa—Biography—Juvenile literature. I. Holland, Gini. II. Title.
III. Graphic biographies.
DT1974.O38   2006
968.06'5092—dc22   2005027855

First published in 2006 by
World Almanac® Library
A Member of the WRC Media Family of Companies
330 West Olive Street, Suite 100
Milwaukee, WI 53212 USA

Copyright © 2006 by World Almanac® Library.

Produced by Design Press, a division of the
Savannah College of Art and Design
Design: Janice Shay and Maria Angela Rojas
Editing: Kerri O'Hern
Illustration: D. McHargue
World Almanac® Library editorial direction: Mark Sachner
    and Valerie J. Weber
World Almanac® Library art direction: Tammy West

Printed in the United States of America

1 2 3 4 5 6 7 8 9 10 09 08 07 06